COLORING with 75 MANDALAS

Copyright© 2021

BOIRETA PUBLISHER

BOÏRETA
PUBLISHER

BOïRETA
PUBLISHER

BOÏRETA
PUBLISHER

BOïRETA
PUBLISHER

BOïRETA
PUBLISHER

BOïRETA
PUBLISHER

BOiRETA
PUBLISHER

BOïRETA
PUBLISHER

BOïRETA
PUBLISHER

BOïRETA
PUBLISHER

BOÏRETA
PUBLISHER

BOïRETA
PUBLISHER

BOïRETA
PUBLISHER

BOïRETA
PUBLISHER

BOïRETA
PUBLISHER

BOïRETA
PUBLISHER

BOïRETA
PUBLISHER

BOïRETA
PUBLISHER

BOÏRETA
PUBLISHER

BOÏRETA
PUBLISHER

BOïRETA
PUBLISHER

BOïRETA
PUBLISHER

BOïRETA
PUBLISHER

BOïRETA
PUBLISHER

BOïRETA
PUBLISHER

BOïRETA
PUBLISHER

BOïRETA
PUBLISHER

BOïRETA
PUBLISHER

BOïRETA
PUBLISHER

BOïRETA
PUBLISHER

BOïRETA
PUBLISHER

BOïRETA
PUBLISHER

BOïRETA
PUBLISHER

BOïRETA
PUBLISHER

BOïRETA
PUBLISHER

BOïRETA
PUBLISHER

BOïRETA
PUBLISHER

BOiRETA
PUBLISHER

BOiRETA
PUBLISHER

BOïRETA
PUBLISHER

BOïRETA
PUBLISHER

BOïRETA
PUBLISHER

BOiRETA
PUBLISHER

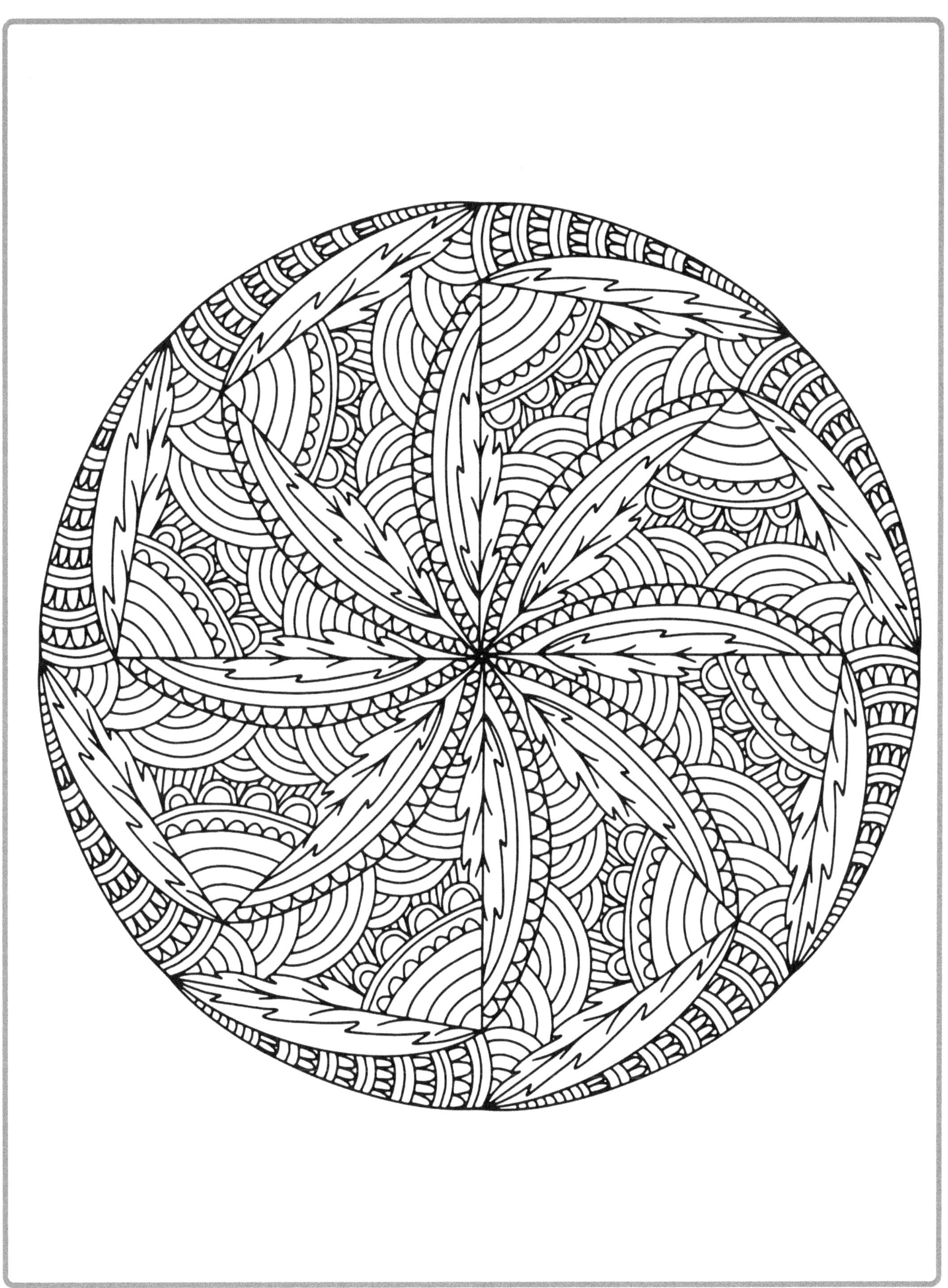

BOÏRETA
PUBLISHER

BOïRETA
PUBLISHER

BOïRETA
PUBLISHER

BOïRETA
PUBLISHER

BOïRETA
PUBLISHER

BOïRETA
PUBLISHER

BOïRETA
PUBLISHER

BOïRETA
PUBLISHER

BOïRETA
PUBLISHER

BOïRETA
PUBLISHER

BOïRETA
PUBLISHER

BOïRETA
PUBLISHER

BOïRETA
PUBLISHER

BOïRETA
PUBLISHER

BOïRETA
PUBLISHER

BOïRETA
PUBLISHER

BOïRETA
PUBLISHER

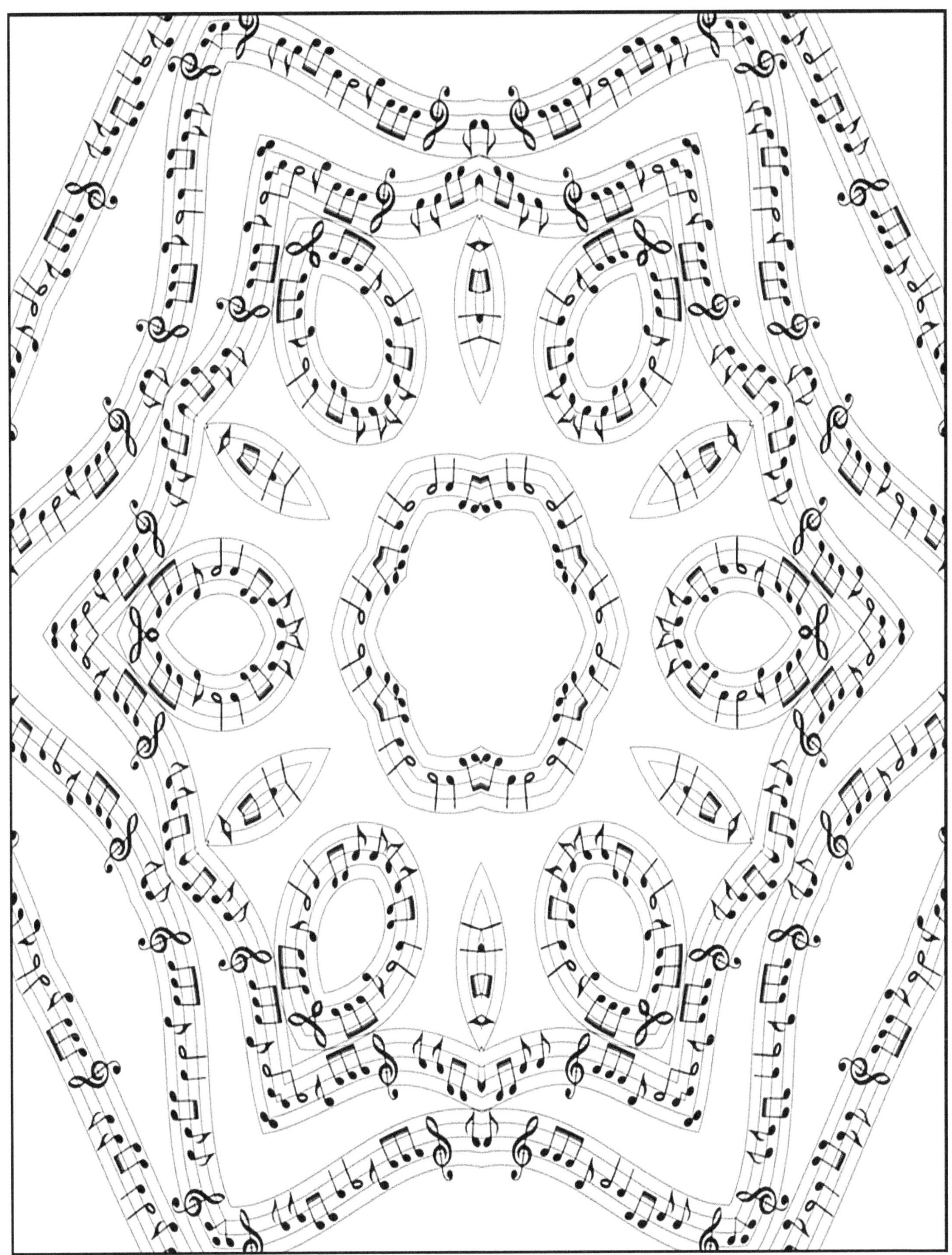

BOÏRETA
PUBLISHER

BOïRETA
PUBLISHER

BOïRETA
PUBLISHER

BOïRETA
PUBLISHER

BOïRETA
PUBLISHER

BOïRETA
PUBLISHER

BOÏRETA
PUBLISHER

THANK YOU

IF YOU ENJOYED THIS COLORING BOOK.
WE WOULD APPRECIATE YOUR POSITIVE
FEEDBACK AND REVIEW!
THAT REALLY HELPS INDEPENDENT AUTHOR

BY BOiRETA PUBLiSHER

TAKE A LOOK AT THE REST OF THE BOOKS WE CAREFULLY DESIGNED BY CLICKING AUTHOR.